# RAISED IN GLORY

The icon of the Resurrection demonstrates the central teaching of the Orthodox Christian faith, depicting Christ, as St. Paul describes "raised in glory" (I Corinthians 15:43), defeating death and liberating the faithful to everlasting life.

# Raised in Glory

## Orthodox Understandings
of
Death, Resurrection, and Immortality

John T. Chirban

HOLY CROSS ORTHODOX PRESS
Brookline, Massachusetts

© Copyright 2002 Holy Cross Orthodox Press
Published by Holy Cross Orthodox Press
50 Goddard Avenue
Brookline, Massachusetts 02445

On the cover: Fragment from *Entrance in Jerusalem, Crucifixion, Anastasis*, Saint Catherine Monastery of Mount Sinai.

LIBRARY OF CONGRESS CATALOGING–IN–PUBLICATION DATA

Chirban, John T.
  Raised in glory and power : Orthodox understand-
ings of death, resurrection, and immortality / John T.
Chirban.
    p. cm.
Includes bibliographical references.
  ISBN 1-885652-62-3 (pbk.)
  1. Death—Religious aspects—Orthodox Eastern
Church. 2. Orthodox Eastern Church—Doctrines. I.
Title.
  BX323 .C48 2002
  236'.1'088219—dc21
                                        2002013103

# Contents

*In Honor of*
*My Mom and Dad*
*Georgia and Thomas Chirban*
*Αἰωνία ἡ μνήμη*

# RAISED IN GLORY

...if Christ had not been raised, then our preaching is
in vain and your faith is in vain. (I Corinthians 15:14)

Death, resurrection, and the afterlife are at the core of
the message of the Orthodox Christian faith. Christianity originates upon the history that Jesus of Nazareth
died on a cross, was resurrected, and ascended into
heaven. These phenomena have direct consequences for
the lives and deaths of all who accept Christ. The Greek
Orthodox Tradition explains the direct relationship between the community of believers and the life, death,
and Resurrection of Jesus Christ in *the* resurrection hymn
sung by the Orthodox faithful during the Easter season:

> Christ has risen from the dead; by death trampling
> upon death; and has bestowed life to those in the
> tomb (Papadeas, G. L., 1979, p. 450).
>
> The Resurrection Service

Orthodoxy's teachings about death point to fundamental beliefs and practices of the faith. One can participate in the conquest of death and "put[s] on immortality," by following the example of Christ Himself (I
Corinthians 15:53). As St. Paul explains:

> For this perishable nature must put on the imper-
> ishable, and this mortal nature must put on immor-
> tality. When the perishable puts on the imperish-
> able and the mortal puts on the immortal, then shall
> come to pass the saying that is written: "Death is

1

swallowed up in victory." "O Hades, where is thy victory?" "O Death, where is thy sting?" The sting of death is sin, and the power of sin is the law. But thanks be to God, who gives us the victory through our Lord Jesus Christ (I Corinthians 15:54-57).

## I. THE MYSTERY OF DEATH

While believers have the promise of emerging victorious from death into eternal life, death remains a mystery. As a "mystery" (with a lower case *m*, meaning "beyond understanding"), death is one of the most challenging and significant issues that each of us must face. Even though death concludes our life cycles, the reality of living and natural fears of mortality render the concept both incomprehensible and painfully mysterious. The unknown nature of death confronts us with a series of paradoxical questions: Does death nullify all we have experienced? Does God await us after death? Should death be preferred over life given its trials and uncertainties? Should we resist our natural inclinations to develop attachments to life, since ultimately they must all be relinquished? How can death give meaning to life? And, where do we go after death?

*Our Relationship with God*

The Orthodox faith attempts to solve this "mystery" through its Mystical Tradition (with an uppercase "M", meaning mystery as a spiritual encounter): *knowledge of God made possible through a paradoxically unknowing, ever-increasing, and continuously enhancing experience.* Within the Mystical Tradition, we understand the depth of God's love through our relationship with Him. By cultivating this relationship over a lifetime, we learn that we are loved ultimately and unconditionally by Him, whose affection is eternal and transcendent, immune to the spatial and temporal constraints and conditions that bind and limit our earthly lives. By experiencing and expressing this love, we promptly understand that this is the same love that motivated Christ's enormous sacrifice, of which it is written: "God so loved the world that he gave his only Son, that whoever believes in him should not perish, but have eternal life" (John 3:16).

*Christ's Answers about Death*

By giving counsel and hope to a lawyer in pursuit of eternal life, Jesus addresses death, asking gently, steering the man to a better understanding.

> ...What is written in the law? How do you read? And he [the lawyer] answered, "You shall love the Lord your God with all your heart, and with all your soul, and with all your strength, and with all your mind: and your neighbor as yourself." And he said to him, "You have answered right; do this and you will live" (Luke 10:26-28).

For Orthodox Christians, the key to eternal life and overcoming the dread of death is to be found in following Christ's commandments to love God, oneself, and others. Implicit in this lesson is the choice of life over death. The Gospel of John records Christ's words: "Truly, truly I say to you, he who hears my word and believes him who sent me, has eternal life; he does not come into judgment, but has passed from death to life" (John 5:24). Elsewhere in the Gospel Jesus says, "...if anyone keeps my word, he will never see death" (John 8:51).

The one who "keeps my word," according to Christ, directs his or her conduct, guided by the love of God toward self and others:

> Then the King will say to those at his right hand, "Come, O blessed of my Father, inherit the kingdom prepared for you from the foundation of the world; for I was hungry, and you gave me food, I was thirsty, and you gave me drink, I was a stranger, and you welcomed me, I was naked, and you clothed me, I was sick, and you visited me, I was in prison, and you came to me." Then the righteous will answer him, "Lord, when do we see thee hungry and feed thee, or thirsty and gave thee drink?...And the King will answer them, "Truly, I say to you, as you did it to one of the least of these my brethren, you did it to me (Matthew 25:34-40).

Therefore, by living a life in concert with Jesus Christ, the mystery of death is solved through the promise of eternal life. The understanding and practices of Orthodox Christians concerning death stem directly from their experiences with Jesus Christ. To explicate further its understanding of death, the Church has established theological teachings that link the traditions of the Orthodox faith with its practices and rituals.

## II. THEOLOGICAL UNDERSTANDINGS ABOUT DEATH

*What is the Connection between Sin and Death?*

Orthodox Christianity teaches that sin introduced death into the universe (Lossky, V., 1973). Sin (from the Greek *amartia*, which literally means "missing the mark") results from what *The Didache*, an early Church treatise, calls choosing the "way of death" over the "way of life." Adam and Eve's original transgression exemplifies the way in which sin severs humanity's relationship with God; it separated them from God. They missed the mark because they freely chose to disobey God. St. Maximos the Confessor says, "Death in the true sense is separation from God ... and this [is] necessarily followed by the body's death" (*The Philokalia*, 1981, p. 81). At the root of death lies sin, and one's separation from God. Therefore, sin is the source, the root of death. Thus, the equation: Sin = separation from God = death.

*Do we choose life or death?*

Sin, and thus death, result from freely choosing a path outside of God – one which is evil. Orthodox teachings assert that God created man neither mortal nor immortal but, as preached by St. Gregory of Nazianzos, capable of attaining either outcome through his or her own exercise of free will or *aftexousion* (Chirban, J., 1986). Death occurs because of our misuse of free will. While God permits free will out of His love for humanity, enabling us to make choices that shape our lives; at the same time, St. Paul explains that sin results in death: "...the wages of sin is death" (Romans 6:23). This is not to say that we can choose not to die by not sinning but that the consequence of our fallen condition, as sinners, is death and that we are essentially dead if we live in sin. Yet hope and salvation are offered by God. Sin is overcome not by human effort alone but by living in Christ and ultimately through God's grace.

In his treatise, *On the Incarnation of the Word*, St. Athanasios explains that Christ:

> took a body like ours, because all our bodies were liable to the corruption of death, He surrendered His body to death in place of all...so that in His death all might die...and the law of death (could be)...fulfilled" (St. Athanasios, 1982, II (7) p. 33).

St. Athanasios explains that Christ's supreme purpose in becoming mortal was the Resurrection: "This was

His victory over death...which is an assurance to all that He had Himself conquered corruption" (St. Athanasios, II (22), p. 52). Christ's coming enabled a fallen humanity to return to God, achieve renewal, and reflect God's image (St. Athanasios, III (14, 16), pp. 41-45).

For Orthodox Christians, *theosis*, deification, and salvation occur when one overcomes sin by following the message of the Resurrection. Moreover, salvation, renewal, resurrection, and *theosis* begin in this life through faith in Jesus Christ, whose Resurrection inaugurated the age of the new creation. The Resurrection of Christ is a triumph over sin and death. Christ's Resurrection inspires His followers to overcome sin by embracing the love that is experienced through communion with one's self, one's neighbors, and God Himself. Christ's personal sacrifice and His message of love transform the cross, a visual emblem of his death, into a symbol of eternal life.

### What Occurs After Death?

Christ's return will herald the dawning of a "new earth" and a "new heaven" where we will undergo a spiritual transformation, and our bodies will become permanently incorruptible. The body will be transfigured, or deified. This transformation relies on a natural, biological event and is not to be understood as magical or mechanical (Nellas, 1987).

The consummation, or redemption, will occur with Christ's glorious return, the resurrection of the dead, and the final Judgment. Because many details concerning death and the process of the resurrection of the dead have not been revealed by God, theologians and scholars offer teachings and opinions based in Holy Tradition that are not doctrinal, called *theologoumena*. For example, while the resurrection of the dead is a doctrinal belief of Orthodox Christians, *theologoumena* are offered to expand on aspects of the afterlife that have not been revealed by God.

## What Happens to the Soul After Death?

Orthodox Christians maintain that the human soul never dies; it is immortal. Our faith determines what will become of our soul. Believers have confidence that their soul lives on with Christ after death, while the faithless, non-believer forfeits the security of this immortal bond. For those who reject Christ, the loss of physical life essentially constitutes "the second death" (Abydos, G., 1997, p. 45). Throughout the Bible we are instructed that the soul remains conscious after death (see references in Luke 16:27-28, Hebrews 2:23, Philippians 1:22, I Peter 3:19, and Revelation 6:9-10). Therefore, once mortal life ends, it is not the soul that sleeps, but the body. This point is inferred from the Gospel of Matthew reports on the Resurrection of Christ:

> the tombs also were opened, and many bodies of the saints who had fallen asleep were raised, and coming out of the tombs after his resurrection they went into the holy city and appeared to many (Matthew 28:52-53).

This *theologoumenon* presents itself as an example of a differing view through its treatment of the subject of the final judgement and the significance of praying for those deceased. According to the theologian Metropolitan Maximos, partial judgment follows physical death and ushers the righteous into an *intermediate stage* of partial blessedness which permits the possibility for this fate of the deceased to be affected by intercessory prayer (Aghiorgoussis, 1999). While this may sound like purgatory, it is not a stage, as in Roman Catholicism, where the souls of those who die may make satisfaction for past sins and earn credits toward heaven.

Memorial services are typically held in the Orthodox Church at intervals of forty days, one year, and ten years, and may be arranged at the discretion of the family of the deceased at other times. While these opportunities primarily support pastoral needs of the family, some theologians and faithful emphasize that such services potentially enhance the fate of the souls of the deceased in gaining forgiveness. Others, again, argue that the fate of the soul is sealed at death, with no possibility of repentance (Danforth, 1982). Professor Christos Androutsos argues that "moral progress" and the eventual redemption of the soul is not possible once it has been separated from the body (Androutsos, 1907, p. 409). Orthodox Christians do not believe in the Roman Catholic teaching of purgatory, where the soul awaits purification before entering heaven, however, many Orthodox Christians believe that "change" remains possible in the intermediate stage after death. For them communication is possible through the prayers of the living (as part of the *militant Church)* and the prayers of the dead (as part of the *triumphant Church*), which may influence one another. This belief explains the importance of praying for the deceased in Orthodox liturgical life. Additionally, alms are often given on behalf of the departed as caring expressions of the family and in honor and support of the deceased; but, as with prayer, there is no suggestion that those who do so can buy salvation as if purchasing indulgences for the remission of sins.

*Will Bodily Resurrection Occur at the Second Coming of Christ?*
In his vision recorded in the Book of Revelation, St

John the Theologian describes what the Kingdom of God will be like when Christ returns:

> Then I saw a new heaven and a new earth, the first heaven and the first earth had passed away and the sea was no more. And I saw the holy city, new Jerusalem, coming down out of heaven from God, prepared as a bride adorned for her husband; and I heard a great voice from the throne saying, "Behold, the dwelling of God is with men. He will dwell with them, and they shall be his people, and God himself will be with them; he will wipe away every tear from their eyes; and death shall be no more death, neither shall there be mourning or crying nor pain any more, for the former things have passed away." And he who sat upon the throne said: "Behold, I make all things new…" (Revelation 21:1-5).

This passage serves as a cornerstone to what Orthodox Christians believe about the Second Coming of Christ. During the funeral service, we read from St. Paul's First Epistle to the Thessalonians:

> But we would not have you ignorant, brethren, concerning those who are asleep, that you may not grieve as others who have no hope. For since we believe that Jesus died and rose again, even so, through Jesus, God will bring with him those who have fallen asleep…. For the Lord himself will descend from heaven and with a cry of command, and with the archangel's call, and with the sound of the trumpet of God. And the dead in Christ will rise first; then we who are alive, who are left, shall be caught up together with them in the clouds to meet the Lord in the air; and so we shall always be with the Lord (1 Thessalonians 4, 13-17).

Bodily death is viewed in Orthodoxy in light of the historical fact that the Kingdom of God was inaugurated through Christ but is not fully manifest on earth. The final judgment is a fundamental belief of the Orthodox faith, which is recorded in the Nicene Creed, in which the faithful profess: "...I expect the resurrection of the dead and the life of Ages to come." This resurrection and transfiguration mark the beginning of a "new creation" (Aghiorgoussis, 1999). Just as the body of Jesus Christ was resurrected, so, too, will all humanity rise up and be restored to a spiritualized existence. The final judgment will occur after humanity's resurrection. Orthodox Christians believe that Jesus Christ will judge us based not only on our sins, but also on our deeds and works of love. Describing the glory of eternal salvation, the Bible counsels us to "wait for new heavens and a new earth, in which righteousness dwells" (II Corinthians 5:10 & II Peter 3:13). At this moment of reckoning, the "end-time," a permanent separation will occur between good and evil, between those who will be awarded an eternal life of happiness in heaven and those who will be condemned to the fires of eternal damnation. The condemned will experience a state of eternal remorse for having rejected God and authentic life in Him (Aghiorgoussis, 1999). Orthodox believers await Christ's return. Therefore, with faith in the Resurrection, ultimately we do not fear death, but rather those who can destroy our soul. Christ says, "And do not fear those who kill the body but cannot kill the soul; rather fear him who can destroy both soul and body in hell" (Matthew 10:28). So, we should not fear death but prepare ourselves to receive it.

As noted, the bodily resurrection of the dead is a basic tenet of the Orthodox faith as outlined by the Nicene Creed. Christ's Resurrection and the bodily resurrection of all humankind are so central to the beliefs of Orthodox Christians that debate is inconceivable. This understanding of the Resurrection embodies so much of the Christian faith that St. Paul asserted:

> If Christ has not been raised, your faith is futile and you are still in your sins (I Corinthians 15:17).

> If in this life we who are in Christ have only hope, we are of all men most to be pitied (I Corinthians 15:19).

Therefore, Christ's Resurrection and our bodily resurrection reflect more than a wish, miracle, or promise. An event that exceeds and surpasses our human comprehension, the bodily resurrection testifies to our union with God, our victory over death, and our living belief in eternal life. Discussing the importance of maintaining one's faith in the face of doubts and skepticism, St. John Chrysostom discusses the consequences of faltering trust in the resurrection at the Second Coming:

> For if we were persuaded that there is no resurrection of bodies, he ("the Devil") would have gradually persuaded them that neither was Christ raised. And thereupon he would also introduce this in due course, that He had not come nor had done what He did (Chrysostom, 1969, p. 266).

Consequently, faith in the promise of the general resurrection of the dead becomes inseparable from faith in Christ Himself. Each implies and necessitates the other.

While Orthodox doctrine insists on Christ's and our own bodily resurrection, it offers little physical or logistical information on the latter process. But, of course, the bodily Resurrection of Christ is described in the

Gospels.[1] It marks the inauguration of this claim. "His appearance was like lightning, and the raiment white as snow...for he has risen... Then go quickly and tell his disciples that he has risen from the dead..." (Matthew 28:3-7).

The importance of codifying such doctrine for our faith is illustrated by the relationships that social values and customs have with theology, and the fact that theological teachings may be influenced by changes in the social climate. For instance, a religious tradition that denies eternal life or dismisses the significance of the body of the dead is less likely to emphasize rites of burial and prayer for the dead. At the same time, a rejection of the immortal soul seems to be in open conflict with those religious and spiritual practices that "scientifically" study (life after death) experiences and seek to prove, empirically, the existence of an afterlife (Moody, 1975). For Orthodox Christians, theological foundations rooted in the earliest Christian communities set the tone for beliefs that take expression in liturgical practice; this, in turn, directly confronts the experience of the dying and bereaved, and leaves us assured but not surprised by scientific accounts of life after death.

The liturgical practice of the faith embodies the theological teachings and serves both to communicate and to express our beliefs about death, the soul, bodily resurrection, and the love of God, as well as to comfort us in times of grief and loss.

### III. LITURGICAL PRACTICE

The liturgical practices in Orthodoxy engage and ac-

---

[1] Note that the Greek word *evangelion*, literally the "Good News" or "Announcement," refers to the announcement of the Resurrection, proclaiming the essence of Christ's story.

tivate all our senses – in body, mind, and soul, in the experience of death. The hymns express gratitude to God for the blessed opportunities of life, focusing particularly on the gift of Christ's sacrifice. Traditional Byzantine chant, drawing from eight tonal variations, powerfully conveys the range of human emotions experienced at death, moving audibly from the depths of sadness (resonated in the lowest, dissonant tones) to the jubilant heights of transcendent joy (captured in the highest tones). Equally symbolic, the burning of incense visually conjures up the image of the incense transporting our prayers to Heaven above with Christ, where the departed finds peace. Lastly, candles symbolize liberation from darkness as the departed embarks on the path to the Light.

*Orthodox Burial – Christ's and Ours*

The liturgical message regarding death and rebirth finds fullest expression in the Good Friday service of Jesus Christ: rebirth is not reincarnation, but resurrection. In this dramatic liturgical event, a multitude of the faithful pray through the night and  commemorate not only the Crucifixion of Jesus Christ but also the loss of the community's deceased. In this liturgical moment, agony, emptiness, and loss are replaced by burgeoning triumph and celebration as the faithful anticipate Christ's Resurrection and the pending resurrection of all who have passed.

Burial customs for Orthodox Christians derive from Gospel accounts in which the apostles prepare Christ's lifeless body. With remarkable congruence, the Gospels describe key elements of the burial including the shroud and the tomb – both of which have become central images in the Orthodox funeral service.

Matthew's Gospel reports,
> And Joseph took the body and wrapped it in a clean linen shroud, and laid it in his own new tomb, which he had hewn in the rock; and he rolled a great stone to the door of the tomb (Matthew 27: 59-60).

Mark's Gospel states,
> Joseph of Arimathea brought a linen shroud and taking him down, wrapped him in the linen shroud, and laid him in the tomb which had been hewn out of the rock; and he rolled a stone against the door of the tomb (Mark 15: 43-46).

Luke's Gospel says,
> Joseph from the Jewish town of Arimathea took [Jesus' body] down and wrapped it in a linen shroud, and laid him in a rock-hewn tomb, where no one had ever been laid  (Luke 23: 50-53).

John's Gospel records,
> They took the body of Jesus, and bound it in linen cloths with the spices…there was a garden, and in the garden a new tomb where no one had ever been laid…they laid Jesus there (John 19: 40-42).

Drawing from the descriptions in these accounts, strikingly visual passages from the Good Friday Vespers and the Lamentations of the Good Friday service convey in emotionally charged and resonant language the physical circumstances of Jesus' death as experienced by those attending to Him:

> O You who puts on light like a robe, when Joseph with Nikodemos brought You down from the Tree and beheld You dead, naked, and unburied, he mourned outwardly and grievously, crying to You

with signs, and saying: Woe is me, sweet Jesus, whom but a while ago, when the sun beheld suspended upon the Cross, it was shrouded in darkness, the earth quaked with fear, and the veil of the Temple was rent asunder. Albeit, I see that You willingly endure death for my sake. How then shall I prepare You, my God? How shall I wrap You with linen? Or what dirges shall I chant for Your funeral? Wherefore, O compassionate Lord, I magnify Your Passion, and praise Your burial with Your Resurrection, crying, Lord, glory to You (Papadeas, p. 360).

Good Friday Vespers

When Joseph of Arimathea took You, the Life of all, down from the Tree, dead; he buried you. Bathing You with sweet and costly myrrh, gently he covered You with fine linen. And with sorrow and tender love in his heart and on his lips, he embraced Your most pure Body and yearned that it may be enshrouded; Wherefore, hiding his fear, he cried to You, rejoicing: Glory to Your condescension, O Merciful Master (Papadeas, p. 359).

Good Friday Lamentation Service

Based on these traditions, the attending clergy who acknowledges the body's sacred role as the Temple of the Holy Spirit, seeks to render the corpse incorruptible by wrapping it in shrouds to prepare for the bodily resurrection. In keeping with ancient practices, priests anoint the body with myrrh and oil; shape a cross over the body, which symbolizes the sacred and good struggles of the departed; and pray to heal the sins of the deceased. At this point, the priest recites, from Psalm 51:7: "Purge me with hyssop... and I shall be clean; wash me and I shall be whiter than snow." Dressed and anointed, the body is positioned in the grave, traditionally facing east, toward the Holy Land, the region of

Christ's ministry, which is believed to be the seat of the final resurrection. Matthew 24:27 reads, "For as lightning comes from the east and shines as far as the west, so will be the coming of the Son of man."

The burial service is as much for the living as for the dead. On behalf of the faithful, the clergy place a handful of dirt within the coffin and recite, "The earth is the Lord's and the fullness thereof...." (Psalm 24:1) "...you are dust, and to dust you shall return" (Genesis 3:19). The custom also invites our participation in the action of the burial – through a personal and emotional interaction of the participants with the deceased.

Even so, referring to those believers for whom proper burial is rendered impossible, St. Augustine assures his reader of God's vigilance in tending to the dead:

> But even though the body has been all quite ground up to powder by some severe accident, or by ruthlessness of enemies, and though it has been so diligently scattered to the winds, or into the water, that there is no trace of it left, yet it shall not be beyond the omnipotence of the Creator – no, not a hair of its head shall perish (St. Augustine, 1969, p. 499).

While God provides for those who have lost their body to war or disaster, the intentionally disruption of a corpse, as in the case of premeditated cremation, is not permitted in the Orthodox Church. For example, in Japan, state law sometimes requires cremation of the dead. But, in cases which are beyond one's control, such as the mandates of state law, resurrection is never threatened, as it lies within the domain of a protective God.

*Iconographic Messages About Death and Resurrection*
    Affirming the importance of the loss of the faithful's loved one, the Orthodox funeral service and the icons

that it employs visually testify to the claim that, "nothing was too good: the finest linen, the most expensive ointment, a brand new tomb" (Sisters of the Orthodox Monastery of the Transfiguration, 1997, p. 25). Dramatic liturgical conventions and symbolically charged iconography express the gut-wrenching and profound agony of loss, as well as the miracle and joy of life anticipated in the promised Resurrection. (See Figures 1, 2, and 3). In both visual and audible art forms, the death of Christ is staged against the backdrop of the Kingdom of God, an ephemeral space in which the past, present, and future – the temporal and the eternal – mingle interchangeably with one another. Experiencing fully the dynamic tension between the tragedy of death, on the one hand, and the miracle and joy of life, on the other, participants give full vent to the range of emotional expression.

The icon of the *Pieta* called the Apokathilosis in Greek (Figure 1), depicts the Mother of God, Mary, mourning over Jesus' body after the Crucifixion. This 15th century Italo-Cretan icon, bordered by angels, whose open hands convey shock and despair, the icon illustrates both heaven and earth grieving over the inconceivable act of destroying the Son of God (Weitzmann, Alibegasuili, Volskaja, Chatzidakis, Babic, Alpatou, & Voinescu, 1982, p. 327). In the late 15th century Russian icon of the *Entombment* (Figure 2), the iconographer captures the grief of a woman, cloaked in red, raising her arms in a gesture of ceremonial incantation. The scene depicts both a natural, human lament for the departed as well as participation in a solemn ritual. Against warm and dull tones of brown and white, the woman's bright red cloak draws the eye of the observer, focusing attention on the icon's central spiritual event (Weitsmann et. al., 1982, p. 285). In an image that brings together the motifs of the *Pieta* and *Entombment*, the late 17th Century Byzantine

## Picture 1
*Pietá*

Monastery of Kechrionos, Cephalonia, 15th century.

Picture 2
*Entombment*

Tretyakov Gallery, Moscow, 15th century.

### Figure 3
*The Epitaphios Threnos*

Holy Transfiguration Monastery, Brookline, Massachusetts.

icon *Epitaphios* (Figure 3), or "tomb," shows the preparation of Christ's body by Joseph of Arimathea. It evokes the words of the Gospels in its depiction of both the cross itself and the linen shroud in which the corpse was wrapped (Weitzmann et. al., p. 327). Liturgical theologian Rev. Alkiviadis Calivas describes the death of Christ as the "true birthday" of the Orthodox Church (1992, p. 64). His comments bring together the ecclesial images of iconography and liturgical practice concerning the message of the Church on death. Reflecting on the thoughts of theologian Boris Bobrinskoy, Calivas says that death takes on a "positive value." Even if physical death continues, it becomes the threshold of the passage from "death to life, rather than from life to death" (p. 242). Calivas continues:

> ... through the Church we appropriate the transforming power of the death and Resurrection of Christ which places upon us the obligation to actualize the renunciations demanded of us by the Gospel in our everyday activities. It calls us to abjure the false values of the fallen world and inspires us to seek after all that is noble, good, natural, and sinless. It encourages us to struggle against all forms of oppression and unjust conditioning which devalue and diminish human life; do more for the life of others in the world; and work for the fulfillment of the Church's vocation in the world (1992, p. 93).

In this way, we see both the connection between the Crucifixion and Resurrection of Christ in our theology and personal lives, and the shared experience – in terms of sadness and joy – in death and rebirth.

*The Funeral Service*
    The purpose of the funeral service is:

- to help us come to a deeper understanding of the meaning and purpose of life;
- to help us cope with our emotions at a time of great loss;
- to recognize the grief that accompanies the loss of a loved one and to encourage expression of our feelings; and
- to celebrate the powerful hope we have as Christians.

Liturgical services alleviate the pain experienced by the loss of a loved one. In response to death, the Orthodox Tradition works to comfort a mourner by declaring the victory of eternal life through Christ's personal sacrifice. Moreover, it attends to particular concerns and experiences of those left behind. The tradition addresses beliefs they have about the death of their loved one and provides details about his or her well-being. We are given graphic images that shapes our perspective of how our spiritual life affects our everyday and future existence:

> O God of spirits and of all flesh, who overcame death and abolished the devil and gave life to your world, the same hand, give rest to the soul of your departed servant (Name) in a place of light, in a place of happiness, in a place of peace, where there is no pain, sorrow, or suffering. Gracious and merciful God, forgive every sin committed by him, whether by word, or deed, or thought. For there is no man who lives and does not sin. You alone are without sin. Your righteousness is eternal and your word is truth (Hatzopoylos, 1985, p. 13).
>
> Prayer from the Funeral Service

Likewise, hymns in the Funeral Service composed by St. John of Damascus offer perspective and consolation to the bereaved:

### First Tone

What pleasure is there in life that has no sorrow? Which glory remains on this earth without change? All is more fleeting than shadow, more elusive than dreams. A sudden change and all of these are followed by death. Yet in this light of your countenance and in the sweetness of your beauty, give rest to the one you have chosen, O Christ, Lover of humanity.

### Fourth Tone

Indeed, the mystery of death is awesome. How the soul is suddenly separated from the harmony of the body. And how the natural bond of being together is cut off by the divine will. So we pray to you: O Life – giver and host of humanity, give rest to the one who departed this life in the company of the just.

### Plagal Fourth Tone

I weep and I wail when I perceive death and see laid in the grave the beauty, fashioned for us in the likeness of God, to be without form, without glory, without beauty. What an amazing thing! What is this mystery that happened around us? How were we delivered to conception and how did we become united with death? Surely, by the will of God who gives to the departed rest (Hatzopoylos 1985, pp. 29-35).

Faith in the power of the Resurrection accounts for the joyful tone and hopeful passages in the funeral rite. This optimism is joined with a communal recognition of grief and loss, manifested in the more saddened, minor key of the hymns. Interwoven, in the Orthodox funeral service are seemingly paradoxical moods, sounds, and actions that simultaneously express concern and empathy for loss in this world, while celebrating faith and joy for eternal life in the next. Commenting on a sermon by St. John Chrysostom on an Epistle to the Thessalonians, St. Augustine explains this dual concept as *hopeful grief.* He points out that, even if we are Christian and anticipate life after death, it is still natural to mourn – yet we are "not to mourn as others who have no hope" (Rutherford, & Barn, 1989, pp. 33-34).[1]

As the greatest link between God and the faithful, prayer serves as a primary medium for the exchange of communication and love between the living and the dead. As such, prayer to or for the deceased affirms and deepens the bonds of the living with the departed. Additionally, the power of prayer establishes a personal, living connection between the dead and mourning and works both to mitigate the pain of loss and support the journey of the immortal soul. All these features are illustrated in the following prayer from the funeral service:

> O Lord of Hosts, who are the consolation of the afflicted, and the comfort of those who mourn; and the succor of all those who are faint-hearted: Comfort through Your Loving-Kindness, those who are distressed with weeping for him (her) who has fallen asleep and heal every pain that does oppress their hearts. And give rest in Abraham's bosom unto Your servant, *(Name),* who has fallen asleep in the hope of resurrection into life eternal. For You are the Resurrection, and the Life, and the Repose of Your servant, *(Name),* Christ our God; and unto You do we ascribe glory, with Your Father who is from everlasting, and Your all-holy and good, and life-giving

---

[1] Also, see St. Gregory of Nazianzos' very powerful illustration of hope in his funeral oration for his brother Basil (St. Gregory, 1968, pp. 27-100).

Spirit, now, and ever, and unto ages of ages. Amen
(Hapgood, 1975, pp. 400-401).

Prayer from the Funeral Service

With solemnity and respect, the faithful approach to
touch and kiss the body, is reverent expression of love
for the deceased. The final kiss underscores the community and communion of the faithful demonstrating
their communal love and grief – living and dead
(Vassiliadis, 1993). Finally, the mourners, symbolically
recreating the Last Supper, join in a traditional meal of
fish, bread, and wine.

## IV. CARE FOR THE DYING AND GRIEVING

*Role of Sacraments*
We have considered how the Orthodox sacramental
tradition creates a personal engagement between the
suffering individual and the greater community. Clergy
embody this connection by presiding over rituals of
mourning. Bridging the gap between the isolated self
and a collective spiritual identity, the clergyman symbolizes the contact between Church and believer. They
unite individuals with a greater, nurturing collectivity
in Holy Confession, Holy Communion, Holy Unction,
and laying of hands. A direct borrowing from Christ's
own ministry, the Orthodox practice of touch resonates
profoundly for those who are dying (Piligian, 1991).

While Orthodox clergy rely upon the liturgical practices of the sacraments in fulfilling their mission, personal
attunement and an adherence to Christ's own approach
in ministry are also essential to the effectiveness of pastoral. Orthodox ministry encompasses a twofold art: to
listen to the dying and bereaved as unique persons, and
to fulfill the sacramental role which facilitates the

parishioner's relationship with God, self, and others.

## Attuning to the Individual

The Church seeks to comfort and console those touched by the experience of death and dying. Preserved through liturgical and theological, the pastoral tradition calls for clerical attunement to one's experience of loss and abandonment. This revitalizes a connection with God and the community during times of crisis and fear. A pastor cannot support such connections through study of Scripture or theory or adherence to ritual alone. Innate compassion and genuine care lie at the core of successful attunement. Effective clergy will observe, listen, and respond to the needs of the grieving and the sick with unrehearsed sensitivity and humane understanding (Chirban, 1996).

While the theological and liturgical traditions of Orthodox Christianity aim to alleviate everyday suffering and preserve access to the Spirit, the art of pastoral care serves to meet the particular needs of community members. In the absence of such care, the individual needs of a distressed layperson may be overshadowed by the observance of rituals that value the collective spirit. The powerful pastoral implications of the Holy Tradition necessitate *application* of the learned wisdom of doctrine. Christ's attunement to those in need (as recorded in Holy Scriptures) serves *par excellence* as examples of insight and discernment.

Holy Scripture portrays Christ as alert to the unique demands of each encounter and crisis. Attunement to an individual's experience of death requires a thoughtful and personal approach to the particular "stage" of that person's grieving. In pursuit of this goal, Orthodox Christian theologians have delineated the implications of applied liturgy (*leiturgia*, in the Greek, literally meaning "work of the people") and, specifically, how it translates into effective care for the individual communicant (Allen, 1979; Chirban, 1985, 1996, 2001; Pharos, 1988).

*Exposing Children to Death Rituals*
   Cultures address children and the topic of death in various ways. In some traditions, death rituals are viewed as natural phenomena in which children actively participate, while others find the idea of exposing children to this process inappropriate and frightening.

While the subject of death may be disturbing, denying a child the opportunity to experience and express his or her feelings about the loss of someone who is beloved may create significant emotional distress. Depriving a child from expressing and understanding his or her feelings, may actually generate fears about death and a host of emotional and physical symptoms.

In American society today, children are exposed to storybook fables of death contrasted with graphic media images which often picture the end of life as violent and disturbing. Our duty as parents is not to protect our children from the reality of death but to nurture them such that they understand death occurs as part of life. Teaching our children about our beliefs concerning death will support their own understanding and ultimately lead to acceptance of this passage in their journey – as well as to deepen understanding of life.

Inevitably, children experience the loss of pets that they valued and about whom they have heartfelt feelings. They ask questions like: Why did my pet die? Where is my pet now? Will I ever get over my sadness? These moments become important for helping the child express and understand his or her feelings. These are formative opportunities to develop the child's notions of self, relationships, God, and beliefs.

Children understand death differently according to their social, intellectual, and psychological development (Chirban, 2002). Psychologists have described various models that can guide what we say and help us to understand what our child is experiencing (Goldman, L., 2002).[1] For example, I recall a little boy who was having difficulty sleeping after the death of his grandfather. Surprisingly no one asked him why he could not sleep. It wasn't until directly discussing the problems of his sleep with the little boy that we learned what was behind his difficulty. He explained, "I don't want to sleep because my mom and dad said that when grandpa went away he was just sleeping and will never wake up again!" The little boy's concrete stage of thinking led him to conclude that because his grandfather was "just sleeping" that when he sleeps maybe he will never wake up either. He did not yet have the abstract thinking abilities to understand metaphor or equate the idea of death as sleep.

While it is true that embracing the powerful and unbridled feelings of a child concerning the death of a loved one may be emotionally demanding and uncomfortable, it should not be *our* difficulty in managing the experiences of our children in times of death which leads us to shelter him or her, thereby avoiding their experience as a means for emotional containment. Only by appropriately participating in life's events can a child develop a realistic and spiritually grounded understanding of life. While it is our duty to protect our children and provide them safety, we cannot shield them from life – which includes understanding death. By helping

[1] Also, see Louis K. Brown's *When Dinosaurs Die*, preschoolers; Dorma O'Toole's *Arnold the Aardvark Finds Hope*, elementary school level; and Marge Heegaard's *When Someone Special Dies*, young teens.)

our children in a manner appropriate to their readiness to confront death we support their process for discovering meaning in their life. By directly encouraging and discussing our child's questions and feelings about death, we may, for example, clarify that God did not create death, or "take one's mother," but that while we do not know enough about death, it is a passage to everlasting peace and joy which is affected by the way we live in Christ.

*Ministering at Death*

We have noted that Church ritual calls for prayer and sacrament for healing, in addition to human contact. When facing the fears of death – its isolation and loneliness – one feels a need to be close to another, to be touched. Vividly exemplified by Christ Himself, physical *presence* at times of suffering works as a balm, providing comfort and healing to the whole person – body, mind and soul.

Death may serve as a barometer of both our faith and our ability to act with a message of compassion. It can act as a call to share in someone else's vulnerability, to contemplate death and, together, to rise above it. It is natural that many shy away from this challenge, avoiding death, illness, and the kind of existential crisis brought about by the initial shock and adjustment to moments of extreme emotional and psychological despair. St. Gregory of Nazianzos describes such despair after the death of his brother, St. Basil:

> You ask how I am…Well, I am very bad. Basil I have no longer; Caesarios I have no longer; the intellectual and physical brothers are both dead. "My father and mother have left me," I can say with David. Physically I am ill, age is descending on my head.

Cares are choking me; affairs oppress me; there is no reliance on friends and the Church is without shepherds. The good is vanishing; evil shows itself in all its nakedness. We are travelling in the dark; there is no lighthouse and Christ is asleep. What can one do? I know only one salvation from these troubles, and this is death. But even the world to come seems terrible to judge by this present world (Campenhausen, 1955, pp. 101-102).

While understandably distraught, this great Father of the Church restabilized himself through prayer and connection with God to emerge from the emotional depths, having grown from this experience and renewing his commitment to his spiritual path (Chirban, 1986). Following the example of St. Gregory, a man who recognized his own fallibility, we must reconcile ourselves with a humble admission of humanity and vulnerability.

The Greek Orthodox understanding of death exists within a broad cultural matrix of attitudes and approaches. Foremost among theorists of modern thanatology has been Dr. Elizabeth Kübler-Ross whose groundbreaking work *On Death and Dying* (1969) outlines five progressive stages commonly experienced in the course of terminal illness: 1) denial or isolation; 2) anger; 3) bargaining; 4) depression; and 5) acceptance. Kübler-Ross' thesis initiated a revolution in medical and psychological literature by tackling a subject that had been carefully avoided in both professional debates and mainstream culture. Furthermore, her work triggered and facilitated a long overdue dialogue between health care providers and the terminally ill patients for whom they worked. Our collective understanding of death and dying has developed considerably in the decades following these breakthroughs. How has the Orthodox Tradition reconciled modern pastoral attitudes with an ever-growing field of psychological study? How has Orthodoxy assimilated its age-old theology with modern understandings of human needs?

Psychological studies have examined closely how the positive impact of the empathy and guidance of a caretaker affect the experience of both the afflicted and their loved ones (S. Bowlby, 1969 and Stern, 1985). Knowledge garnered from such study is vital to the improvement of Orthodox pastoral care. Bolstered by research in death, bereavement, and the readiness to integrate belief with modern understandings of psychology, the clergy can better care for laypersons in distress (Byock, 1997; Field, & Cassel, Eds., 1997; Kastenbaum, & Aisenberg, 1996; Rando, 1984; Rando, Ed., 2000).

At the same time, it is noted that studies that are exclusively scientific in nature often overlook the extent to which faith may influence the prognosis of a terminally ill patient or the outlook of an afflicted loved one. For example, while Kübler-Ross identifies five stages of death and dying, her pioneering book did not adequately examine the role of faith in each of them. She overlooks a range of intense spiritual experiences that frequently accompany periods of grief. When she does acknowledge the impact of religious healing, Kubler-Ross arrives at a telling conclusion:

> Truly religious people with a deep, abiding relationship with God have found it easier to face death with equanimity. We do not often see them because they aren't troubled, so they don't need our help (Kübler-Ross, 1974, p. 163).

From this perspective, one's faith serves a positive and preventative role in mental health. But is this an adequate view of how a faithful person experiences death?

Acceptance, the final stage in her model, represents a point of resignation rather than a positive, ideal approach to mortality. Kübler-Ross clearly articulates this distinction, warning that:

> Acceptance should not be mistaken for a happy stage. It is almost void of feelings. It is as if the pain had gone, the struggle is over, and there comes a time for the 'final rest before the long journey' as one patient phrased it... (Kübler-Ross, 1969, p. 100).

Strict adherence to this model fails to explain the enlightened experiences of many exemplary Christian figures. For instance, when St. Ignatios of Antioch desired to die for Christ, he demonstrated neither fearful denial nor neutral acceptance of death. He espoused instead a transcendent view of mortality that escapes this clinical categorization. As the second bishop of Antioch, St. Ignatios was sentenced to death during the reign of Emperor Trajan (98-117 AD) and condemned to be devoured by wild beasts. In the face of this horrific demise, St. Ignatios shocked his contemporaries, begging that his life not be spared. Driven by an ardent desire to die for Christ, St. Ignatios embraced death. For him it heralded the beginning of true life:

> At last I am on the way to being a disciple. May nothing seen or unseen fascinate me, so that I may happily make my way to Jesus Christ! Fire, cross, struggles with wild beasts, wrenching of bones, mangling of limbs, crushing of the whole body, cruel tortures inflicted by the devil – let them come upon me, provided only I make my way to Jesus Christ. Of no use to me be the farthest reaches of the universe or the Kingdoms of this world. I would rather die and come to Jesus Christ than be the King over

the entire earth. Him I seek who died for us; Him I love who rose again because of us. The birth pangs are upon me. Forgive me, brother; do not obstruct my coming to life – do not wish me to die; do not make a gift to the world of one who wants to be God's. Beware of seducing me with matter; suffer me to receive pure light. Once arrived there I shall be a man (Romans 5:3-6) – Why, moreover, did I surrender myself to death, to fire, to the sword, to wild beasts? Well, to be near the sword is to be near God; to be in the claws of wild beasts is to be in the hands of God. Only let it be done in the name of Jesus Christ! To suffer with Him I endure all things, if He, who became perfect man, gives me the strength (Quasten, 1966, p. 71).

St. Ignatios' experience with and experience for death can not adequately understood through Kübler-Ross' stages of denial or acceptance. St. Ignatios' faith is not wishful but, rather, rests on the power of living faith – faith as reality. Pastoral care requires a particular attunement and understanding of the many elements which informs the individual dying or bereaved's response to death. Only through comprehensive understanding of the various elements that inform someone's experience can we effectively respond.

*The Monastic Tradition*
      Understanding death and reflecting upon its Mystery allows us to value life. Our Church places great emphasis upon the study of meditation on death. Through such reflection one approaches the deeper meanings and experiences of faith, hope, and love. In contemplating death, one registers the shortness and fragility of this life and is led to depend instead *on the life of Christ*. St. Philotheos of Sinai captures this senti-

ment when he asserts, "ceaseless mindfulness of death purifies intellect and body to understand true life" (Nikodimos of the Holy Mountain & Makarios of Corinth, 1983, p. 17).

The monastic tradition developed a rigorous practice for strengthening the soul, from which most forms of spiritual meditation are currently drawn. "Detachment from material things," as St. Peter of Damaskos wrote:

> gives rise to the contemplation of spiritual realities – contemplation not of created beings in this present life, but of the awesome things that take place before and after death. For the detached person is taught about these things by grace, so through inward grief he may mortify the passions and, when the time is ripe, attain peace and gentleness in his thoughts (Nikodimos & Makarios, 1983, p. 231).

As depicted in this passage, spiritual growth arises from our capacity to move beyond all material things. The practice of spiritual asceticism prescribed by St. Peter of Damasksos requires a controlled detachment

> ... not only over external things, but also over the body, through our non-attachment to it, and over death, through the courage of our faith; then in the life to come we shall reign in our bodies externally with Christ, through the grace of the general resurrection (Nikodimos & Makarios, 1983 p. 125).

Within the framework of Orthodoxy exists a broad array of spiritual recommendations, ranging from conservative mandates (by which we denounce all that is material to discover our soul) to more liberal ideologies (by which we are instructed to embrace the attachments of this world, recognizing through them the teachings and sacrifices of Christ). From among these the believer must choose his or her path through which he or she will find fulfillment and salvation.

*Hope*

Hope is needed at no time more than at the moment in which we confront death. Hope is not only a living virtue of faith but also an eager anticipation of the promised Kingdom which Christ inaugurated, at a time and place that is both "now and not yet" realized. While modern research demonstrates the power of hope, optimism, and faith in the regular maintenance of one's health and well-being (Koenig, Pargament, & Nielsen, 1998; Levin, & Vanderpool, 1991; Sethi, & Seligman, 1993), these psychological values take on a new and urgent set of meanings when embraced by the dying believer. Faced with mortality, Orthodox Christians look forward to the communion with God to which their hope testifies and trust in the truth of life after death. For example, St. Ignatios equates Holy Communion with the "medicine of immortality, and the sovereign remedy by which we escape death and live in Jesus Christ for evermore" (Rutherford, & Barn, 1989, p. 7). In both liturgy and personal life, hope is perhaps the deepest expression of one's faith, it represents both confidence in one's life today and belief in the promise of immortality. There are times, however, when a Christian does not feel hope at the time of death, but is overcome by feelings of doubt, despair, or fear. Nonetheless, a sense of abiding faith resides within the institutions of the Church, which exists most importantly to support the faithful in such crisis. Support for hope is embodied in the stories of saints and martyrs, all of which testify to the redemptive value of trust in Christ.

A number of Orthodox pastoral guides address the importance of hope for those in the throes of loss (Coniaris, 1969, 1978, 1992; Papakostas, 1967; Pharos, 1981). Father Anthony Coniaris delivers the message of hope as one of faith in the "transfiguration of Christ," a concept closely aligned with Orthodox understandings of death:

> He did not come to teach us to accept suffering and death because they are universal. He did not come to tell us that death is God's will for us. He came to tell us that death was something evil; something not part of God's plan; something that needed to be destroyed. And he destroyed it for us. He gave us the victory. This is why for the Christian the final stage of life cannot be the passive acceptance of death, but its transfiguration in Christ! (1978, p. 27)

By highlighting Christ's role as a "destroyer" of death and a "bringer of victory," Reverend Coniaris enjoins the dying to confront death actively rather than submitting passively to its power. This instructive paradigm for Orthodox Christians finds its precedent in a description, based in Scripture, of believers as "nightwatch people" (Rutherford & Barn, 1989, p. 7), waiting expectantly for the return of the risen Lord (Matthew 28:1; Mark 16:2; Luke 23:50-56; Luke 24:1; John 20:1). This description encompasses the experience of the thousands of martyrs who willingly served as human torches. They endured the cruelest of physical punishments and triumphed over death. Victorious and stoic in the face of their oppressors, these believers maintained their hope and faith in Christ.

## V. REFLECTIONS

Conceptualizing death as the gateway into fuller

communion with God, Orthodox believers are continuously preparing for this spiritual journey. Drawing from the teachings and practices of the Mystical Tradition, believers build their knowledge and faith, heightening their capacity to care and their love for God, self, and others. While many details about death remain a mystery, Orthodoxy professes that by living the precepts and the examples of Christ, one gains confidence in the Resurrection and hope in the infinite love of God, which ultimately renders our death as a fearless time of transition.

Faith in Christ is more than a supplementary, alternative medicine; it dramatically affects the way we live our lives, the way we perceive and experience this existence as well as the next. By demystifying a frightening biological process, the truth of Christ's life transforms death for us. For Orthodox Christians, death is not a final stage but, rather, a transition, leading us toward resurrection. The Orthodox theologian Alexander Schmemann is helpful when he refers the faithful to the example of the disciples to understand how Christians approach life and death:

> The *great joy* that the disciples felt when they saw the risen Lord, that "burning of heart" that they experienced on the way to Emmaus, was not because the mysteries of an "other world" were revealed to them, but because they saw the Lord. And He sent them to… proclaim not the resurrection of the dead – not a doctrine of death – but repentance and remission of sins, the new life, and Kingdom. They announced what they knew, that in Christ this *new life* had already begun, that He is the Life Eternal, the Fulfillment, the Resurrection, and the Joy of the World (Schmemann, 1973, p. 97).

For the Greek Orthodox believer, death, as a stage of our journey, actually clarifies life, orienting our relationship towards God, ourselves, and others. Death is a transition from this fallen world to the Kingdom of God. From the funeral service, we pray "mercifully vouchsafe, O Good One, that he (she) who from this transitory, unstable thing of corruption has passed over unto You, may dwell with joy in the heavenly mansions, O God, being justified by faith and by grace."

The love of God, epitomized in Christ's unconditional love of others, Incarnation, Ministry, Crucifixion, and Resurrection, serves not only as the model for our fulfilling life, but as the key to the door of Eternal Life. Orthodoxy challenges us to recognize and respond to death that surrounds us in its many forms. Moreover, Orthodoxy invites us to participate in the miracle of the Resurrection that confounds death. By living in Christ, the possession of internal Joy manifests itself as Eternal Life.

"Death where is your sting?"

## SELECTED SCRIPTURAL VERSES

## Grieving

*Psalm 102*

A prayer of one afflicted, when he is faint and pours out his complaint before the LORD.

Hear my prayer, O LORD; let my cry come to thee!

Do not hide thy face from me in the day of my distress! Incline thy ear to me; answer me speedily in the day when I call!

For my days pass away like smoke, and my bones burn like a furnace.

My heart is smitten like grass, and withered; I forget to eat my bread.

Because of my loud groaning my bones cleave to my flesh.

I am like a vulture of the wilderness, like an owl of the waste places;

I lie awake, I am like a lonely bird on the housetop.

All the day my enemies taunt me, those who deride me use my name for a curse.

For I eat ashes like bread, and mingle tears with my drink,

because of thy indignation and anger; for thou hast taken me up and thrown me away.

My days are like an evening shadow; I wither away like grass.

But thou, O LORD, art enthroned for ever; thy name endures to all generations.

Thou wilt arise and have pity on Zion; it is the time to favor her; the appointed time has come.

For thy servants hold her stones dear, and have pity on her dust.
The nations will fear the name of the LORD, and all the kings of the earth thy glory.
For the LORD will build up Zion, he will appear in his glory;
he will regard the prayer of the destitute, and will not despise their supplication.
Let this be recorded for a generation to come, so that a people yet unborn may praise the LORD:
that he looked down from his holy height, from heaven the LORD looked at the earth,
to hear the groans of the prisoners, to set free those who were doomed to die;
that men may declare in Zion the name of the LORD, and in Jerusalem his praise,
when peoples gather together, and kingdoms, to worship the LORD.
He has broken my strength in mid-course; he has shortened my days.
"O my God," I say, "take me not hence in the midst of my days, thou whose years endure throughout all generations!"
Of old thou didst lay the foundation of the earth, and the heavens are the work of thy hands.
They will perish, but thou dost endure; they will all wear out like a garment. Thou changes them like raiment, and they pass away;
but thou art the same, and thy years have no end.
The children of thy servants shall dwell secure; their posterity shall be established before thee.

*Psalm 116:1-19*
I love the LORD, because he has heard my voice and my supplications.

Because he inclined his ear to me, therefore I will call on him as long as I live.

The snares of death encompassed me; the pangs of Sheol laid hold on me; I suffered distress and anguish.

Then I called on the name of the LORD: "O LORD, I beseech thee, save my life!"

Gracious is the LORD, and righteous; our God is merciful.

The LORD preserves the simple; when I was brought low, he saved me.

Return, O my soul, to your rest; for the LORD has dealt bountifully with you.

For thou hast delivered my soul from death, my eyes from tears, my feet from stumbling;

I walk before the LORD in the land of the living.

I kept my faith, even when I said, "I am greatly afflicted";

I said in my consternation, "Men are all a vain hope."

What shall I render to the LORD for all his bounty to me?

I will lift up the cup of salvation and call on the name of the LORD,

I will pay my vows to the LORD in the presence of all his people.

Precious in the sight of the LORD is the death of his saints.

O LORD, I am thy servant; I am thy servant, the son of thy handmaid. Thou hast loosed my bonds.

I will offer to thee the sacrifice of thanksgiving and call on the name of the LORD.

I will pay my vows to the LORD in the presence of all his people,

in the courts of the house of the LORD, in your midst, O Jerusalem. Praise the LORD!

## Faith

*Matthew 10: 28-33*

And do not fear those who kill the body but cannot kill the soul; rather fear him who can destroy both soul and body in hell.

Are not two sparrows sold for a penny? And not one of them will fall to the ground without your Father's will.

But even the hairs of your head are all numbered.

Fear not, therefore; you are of more value than many sparrows.

So every one who acknowledges me before men, I also will acknowledge before my Father who is in heaven;

but whoever denies me before men, I also will deny before my Father who is in heaven.

*John 11:25-26*

Jesus said to her, "I am the resurrection and the life; he who believes in me, though he die, yet shall he live,

and whoever lives and believes in me shall never die. Do you believe this?"

## Hope

*Romans 8: 24-28*

For in this hope we were saved. Now hope that is seen is not hope. For who hopes for what he sees?

But if we hope for what we do not see, we wait for it with patience.

Likewise the Spirit helps us in our weakness; for we do not know how to pray as we ought, but the Spirit himself intercedes for us with sighs too deep for words.

And he who searches the hearts of men knows what

is the mind of the Spirit, because the Spirit intercedes for the saints according to the will of God.

We know that in everything God works for good with those who love him, who are called according to his purpose.

*I Thessalonians 4: 13-17*
But we would not have you ignorant, brethren, concerning those who are asleep, that you may not grieve as others do who have no hope.

For since we believe that Jesus died and rose again, even so, through Jesus, God will bring with him those who have fallen asleep.

For this we declare to you by the word of the Lord, that we who are alive, who are left until the coming of the Lord, shall not precede those who have fallen asleep.

For the Lord himself will descend from heaven with a cry of command, with the archangel's call, and with the sound of the trumpet of God. And the dead in Christ will rise first;

then we who are alive, who are left, shall be caught up together with them in the clouds to meet the Lord in the air; and so we shall always be with the Lord.

## Love

*I John 3: 14-16*
And as Moses lifted up the serpent in the wilderness, so must the Son of man be lifted up,

that whoever believes in him may have eternal life."

For God so loved the world that he gave his only Son, that whoever believes in him should not perish but have eternal life.

*I John 4: 14-21*

but whoever drinks of the water that I shall give him will never thirst; the water that I shall give him will become in him a spring of water welling up to eternal life."

The woman said to him, "Sir, give me this water, that I may not thirst, nor come here to draw."

Jesus said to her, "Go, call your husband, and come here."

The woman answered him, "I have no husband."

Jesus said to her, "You are right in saying, `I have no husband';

for you have had five husbands, and he whom you now have is not your husband; this you said truly."

The woman said to him, "Sir, I perceive that you are a prophet.

Our fathers worshiped on this mountain; and you say that in Jerusalem is the place where men ought to worship."

Jesus said to her, "Woman, believe me, the hour is coming when neither on this mountain nor in Jerusalem will you worship the Father.

### Death

*I Corinthians 15: 11-22*

Whether then it was I or they, so we preach and so you believed.

Now if Christ is preached as raised from the dead, how can some of you say that there is no resurrection of the dead?

But if there is no resurrection of the dead, then Christ has not been raised;

if Christ has not been raised, then our preaching is in vain and your faith is in vain.

We are even found to be misrepresenting God, because we testified of God that he raised Christ, whom he did not raise if it is true that the dead are not raised. For if the dead are not raised, then Christ has not been raised.

If Christ has not been raised, your faith is futile and you are still in your sins.

Then those also who have fallen asleep in Christ have perished.

If for this life only we have hoped in Christ, we are of all men most to be pitied.

But in fact Christ has been raised from the dead, the first fruits of those who have fallen asleep.

For as by a man came death, by a man has come also the resurrection of the dead.

For as in Adam all die, so also in Christ shall all be made alive.

*II Corinthians 5: 6-10*

So we are always of good courage; we know that while we are at home in the body we are away from the Lord,

for we walk by faith, not by sight.

We are of good courage, and we would rather be away from the body and at home with the Lord.

So whether we are at home or away, we make it our aim to please him.

For we must all appear before the judgment seat of Christ, so that each one may receive good or evil, according to what he has done in the body.

SELECTED PRAYERS

*From the Funeral Services*

With the righteous souls who are departed give rest to the soul of your servant, O Savior. Guard him in the blessed life, which is from you, O Lover of man.

In your peace, O Lord, where all your saints repose, give rest also to the soul of your servant, for you alone are immortal.

You are our God, who descended into Hades and delivered from their suffering those who are bound there; Give Rest, O Savior, also to the soul of your servant.

The only pure and immaculate Virgin, who gave birth to Christ God, intercede for the salvation of the soul of your servant.

O God of spirits and of all flesh, who overcame death and abolished the devil and gave life to your world, the same Lord, give rest to the soul of your departed servant [(N.)] in a place of light, in a place of happiness, in a place of peace, where there is no pain, sorrow, and suffering. Gracious and merciful God, forgive every sin committed by him, whether by word, or deed, or thought. For there is no man who lives and does not sin. You alone are without sin. Your righteousness is eternal and your word is truth.

What pleasure is there in life that has no sorrow? Which glory remains on this earth without change? All is more fleeting than shadow, more elusive than dreams. A sudden change and all of these are followed by death. Yet, in the light of your countenance and in the sweetness of your beauty, give rest to the one you have chosen, O Christ, Lover of man.

Man withers like a flower and passes like a dream and every man comes to an end. And when the strumpet will sound again the dead will rise like in a quake to greet you, O Christ God. At that time, grant, O Lord, that the one you have taken from us, the soul of your servant, be in fellowship with your saints.

Alas, what a battle for the soul, as it parts from the body! How it weeps, then, and there is no one to help it! It turns its eyes to the angels but it pleads without success. It turns its arms to its fel- [p.31] low men and there is no helping hand. Beloved brothers, let us then consider how short our life is and let us pray to Christ to grant rest to the one departed and to grant our souls the infinite mercy of God.

All is vanity in human affairs; all that cannot be enjoyed after death. No wealth is kept; no glory can follow. For once death has come, all of these are lost. Let us say, therefore, to Christ the Immortal King: Give rest to the one departed where the blessed live.

Indeed, the mystery of death is awesome. How the soul is suddenly separated from the harmony on the body. And how the natural bond of being together is cut off by the divine will. So we pray to you: O Life-giver and Lover of man, give rest to the one departed this life in the company of the just.

Where is the desire of the world? Where is the fantasy of temporary things? Where are the gold [p.33] and the silver? Where is the gathering and noise of friends? All is dust, all is ashes, all is shadow. But let us come to pray to the Immortal King: O Lord, deem the one departed from us worthy of your eternal blessings and give him rest in the everlasting happiness of heaven.

I weep and I wail when I perceive death and see laid in the grave the beauty, fashioned for us in the likeness of God, to be without form, without glory, without beauty. What an amazing thing! What is this mystery that happened around us? How were we delivered to corruption and how did we become united with death? Surely, by the will of God who gives to the departed rest.

# BIBLIOGRAPHY

[Scriptural references are taken from the Revised Standard Version (RSV) of the Holy Bible].

Abydos, G. (1997). *At the end of time: The eschatological expectations of the Church.* Brookline, MA: Holy Cross Press.

Aghiorgoussis, M. (1999). *In the image of God: Studies in scripture, theology, and community.* Brookline, MA: Holy Cross Press.

Allen, J. J. (1979). The Orthodox pastor and the dying. *St. Vladimir's Theological Quarterly.* pp. 23-35.

Androutsos, C. (1907). *Dogmatics.* Athens, Greece.

Athanasios, St. (1982). Religious of CSMV. *On the incarnation of the word.* London: A. R. Mowbray & Co.

Augustine, St. (1969). "The City of God" 22:21. *Nicene and Post-Nicene Fathers, First Series, Volume II.* Quoted from the Sisters of the Orthodox Monastery of the Transfiguration, 1999, *Bodily Resurrection.* Ben Lomond, CA: Conciliar Press.

Bobrinskoy, B. (1979). Old age and death: Tragedy or blessing? *St. Vladimir's Theological Quarterly*, pp. 232-244.

Bowlby, J. (1969). *Attachment and loss: Vol. 1. Attachment.* New York: Basic Books.

Byock, I. R. (1997). *Dying well: The prospect for growth at the end of life.* New York: Riverhead Books.

Calivas, A. (1992). *Great week and Pascha in the Greek Orthodox Church.* Brookline, MA: Holy Cross Orthodox Press.

Callinicos, C. (1969). *Beyond the grave.* Scranton, PA: Christian Orthodox Editions.

Campenhausen, H. (1955). *The fathers of the Greek Church.* New York: Pantheon.

Cavadas, A. (1988). *The world beyond the grave or the after life.* Translated by C. Andrews. Brookline, MA: Holy Cross Orthodox Press.

Chirban, J. T. (2002). Being present for children in tragedy and trauma. *Praxis;* III, 1; pp.33-35.

Chirban, J. T. (Ed.), (1985). *Coping with death and dying: An interdisciplinary approach.* Lanham, MD: University Press of America.

Chirban, J. T. (1986). Developmental stages in Orthodox Christianity. In K. Wilbur, J. Engler, & D. P. Brown (Eds.), *Transformations of consciousness: Conventional and contemplative perspectives on development.* Boston: New Science Library Shambala.

Chirban, J. T. (1996). *Interviewing in depth: The interactive-relational approach.* Thousand Oaks, CA: Sage Publications.

Chirban, J. T. (Ed.), (2001). *Sickness or sin? Spiritual discernment and differential diagnosis.* Brookline, MA: Holy Cross Press.

Chrysostom, St. John (1969). Homilies on First Corinthians. Schaff, P. (Ed.), *Nicene and post-Nicene fathers.* Grand Rapids, MI: Eerdmans, First Series, Volume XII.

Coniaris, A. M. (1969). *61 talks for Orthodox funerals.* Minneapolis, MN: Light and Life Publishing Company.

Coniaris, A. M. (1978). *Christ's comfort for those who sorrow: Messages of hope for those who have lost loved ones.* Minneapolis, MN: Light and Life Publishing Company.

Coniaris, A. M. (1992). *Surviving the loss of a loved one.* Minneapolis, MN: Light and Life Publishing Company.

Constantelos, D. (1991). The interface of medicine and religion. In J. T. Chirban (Ed.), *Health and faith: Medical, psychological and religious dimensions.* Lanham, MD: University Press of America.

Danforth, L. M. (1982). *The death rituals of rural Greece.* Princeton, NJ: Princeton University Press.

Field, M., & Cassel, C. (Eds.), (1997). *Approaching death: Improving care at the end of life.* Washington, D. C: National Academy Press.

Goldman, L. (2002). "Children grieve too." *Dying, death, and bereavement,* Sixth Edition. Guilford, CT: McGraw-Hill/Dushkin, p. 188.

Gregory of Nazianzos, St. and St. Ambrose (1968). *Funeral orations.* Translated by Leo P. McCauley. Washington, DC: Catholic University Press.

Gregory of Nazianzos. *Oration.* 45, 8, P636, 633A. Quoted from the Sisters of the Orthodox Monastery of the Transfiguration, 1999. *Bodily Resurrection.* Ben Lomond, CA: Conciliar Press.

Hapgood, I. F. (1975). *Service book of the holy Orthodox-Catholic apostolic church.* Englewood, NJ: Antiochian Orthodox Christian Archdiocese.

Harakas, S. (1990). *Health and medicine in the Eastern Orthodox tradition.* NY: Crossroad.

Hatzopoylos, H. P. (Ed.), (1985). *Funeral services according to the rite of the Greek Orthodox Church.* Boston, MA: Harry P. Hatzopoylos.

Karmiris, J. (1957). *Synopses Tes dogmetikes didaskalios tes Orthodoxou Catholikos Ekklesesis.* Athens, Greece: The Theological School, Athens University.

Kastenbaum, R., & Aisenberg, R. (1976). *The psychology of death.* New York: Springer Publishing Company.

Kesich, V. (1982). *The first day of the new creation: The Resurrection and the Christian faith.* Crestwood, NY: St. Vladimir's Seminary Press.

Koenig, H. G., Pargament, K. I., & Nielsen, J. (1998). Religious coping and health status in medically ill, hospitalized older adults. *Journal of Nervous and Mental Disease, 18,* 513-521.

Kübler-Ross, E. (1969). *On death and dying: What the dying have to teach doctors, nurses, clergy, and their own families.* London: The Macmillan Company.

Kübler-Ross, E. (1974). *Questions and answers on death and dying.* New York: Collier Books.

Levin, J. S., & Vanderpool, H. I. (1991). Religious factors in physical health and the prevention of illness. *Prevention in Human Services, 9,* 41-64.

Lossky, V. (1973). *The mystical theology of the Eastern Church.* Cambridge, England: James Clarke & Co. Ltd.

Moody, R. A. (1975). *Life after life.* New York: Bantam Books.

Nellas, P. (1987). *Deification in Christ: The nature of the human person.* Crestwood, NY: St. Vladimir's Seminary Press.

Nikodimos of the Holy Mountain (Ed.)., (1962). *Philokalia.* Revised by Theophan the Recluse. Translated by E. Kadloubovsky, & G. E. H. Palmer. Introduction by H. A. Hodges. London, England: Faber & Faber.

Nikodimos of the Holy Mountain and Makarios of Corinth. (Ed.). (1983). *The Philokalia: The complete text.* Volume Two. Translated from the Greek and Edited by G. E. H. Palmer, P. Sherrard, & K. Ware. London, England: Faber & Faber.

Papadeas, G. L. (Ed.), (1979). *Greek Orthodox Holy Week and Easter services.* Daytona Beach, FL: G. Papadeas.

Papakostas, S. (1967). *For the hours of pain.* Translated by L. J. Newville. Athens, Greece: ZOE Brotherhood of Theologians.

Pharos, P. (1981). *To Penthos.* Athens, Greece.

Piligian, K. (1991). Therapeutic touch: Using your hands for help or heal. In Chirban, J. T. (Ed)., *Health and faith: Psychological and religious dimensions.* Lanham, MD: University Press of America.

Plante, T. G., & Sherman, A. C. (2001). *Faith and healing psychology: Exploring the impact on health of religion and spirituality.* NY: Guilford Publications.

Quasten, J. (1966). *Patrology I: The beginnings of patristic literature.* Utrecht-Antwags: Spectrum Press.

Rando, T. A. (2000). *Clinical dimensions of anticipatory mourning: Theory and practice in working with the dying, their loved ones, and their caretakers.* Champaign, IL: Research Press.

Rando, T. A. (1984). *Grief, dying, and death: Clinical interviews for caregivers.* Champaign, Il: Research Press.

Rutherford, R., & Barn, T. (1989). *The death of a Christian: The order of Christian funerals.* Collegeville MN: The Liturgical Press.

Schmemann, A. (1973). *For the life of the world: Sacraments and Orthodoxy.* Crestwood, NY: St. Vladimir's Press.

Sethi, S., & Seligman, M. E. P. (1993). Optimism and fundamentalism. *Psychological Science, 4,* 256-259.

Sherrard, P. (1998). *Christianity: Lineaments of a Sacred Tradition.* Foreword by K. Ware. Brookline, MA: Holy Cross Press.

Sisters of the Orthodox Monastery of the Transfiguration. (1997). *Bodily resurrection.* Ben Lomond, CA: Conciliar Press.

Stern, D. (1985). *The interpersonal world of the infant: A view from psychoanalysis and developmental psychology.* New York: Basic Books.

Vassiliadis, N. P. (1993). Translated by P. Chamberas. *The mystery of death.* Athens, Greece: The Orthodox Brotherhood of Theologians.

Weitzmann, K., Alibegosvili, G., Volskaja, A., Chantzidakis, M., Babie, G., Alpatov, M., & Voimescu, T. (1982). *The icon.* NY: Alfred A. Knopf.

Zeligs, R. (1974). *Children's experience with death.* Springfield, IL: Charles C. Thomas Publishers.